The Mini Book of

Anime

Mitchiri Neko

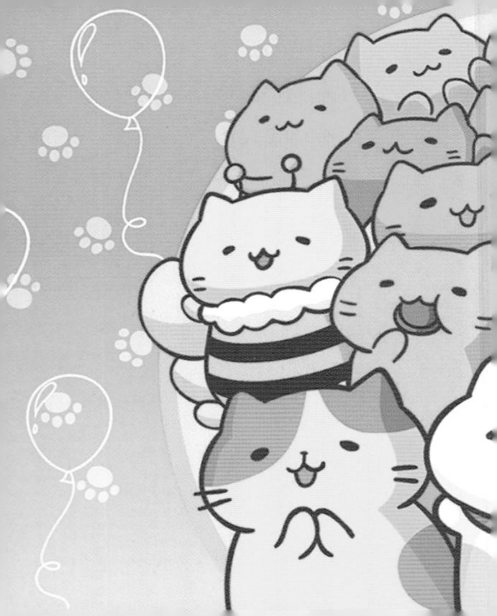

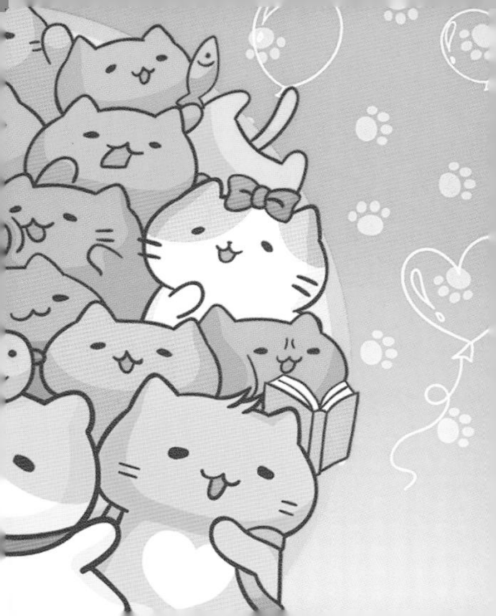

RP Minis™
Hachette Book Group
1290 Avenue of the Americas, New York, NY 10104
www.runningpress.com
@Running_Press

First Edition: September 2020

Published by RP Minis, an imprint of Perseus Books, LLC, a subsidiary of
Hachette Book Group, Inc. The RP Minis name and logo is a trademark of
the Hachette Book Group.

The Hachette Speakers Bureau provides a wide range of authors for
speaking events. To find out more, go to www.hachettespeakersbureau.com
or call (866) 376-6591.

The publisher is not responsible for websites (or their content)
that are not owned by the publisher.

ISBN: 978-0-7624-9800-0

Contents

Hello, Mitchiri Neko!

Every day with Mitchiri Neko is filled with care-free adventures, surreal laughs, and friends!

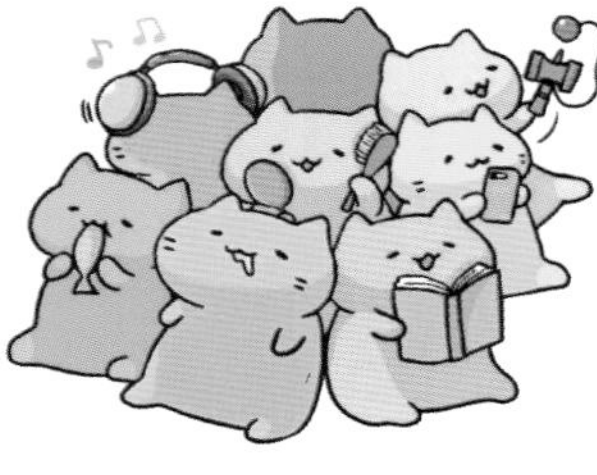

Based on the manga by Frencel, these cat-like creatures always find a way of sticking together when you leave them alone. Whether they are dancing, getting stuck in boxes, being rolled up as sushi, or playing music in a marching band, Mitchiri Neko know how to have a good time.

- The director of *Mitchiri Neko*, *Kyou* Yatate, also works on another adorable anime about cat characters: *Bananya!*

- Mitchiri Neko translates into "Squished Cats."

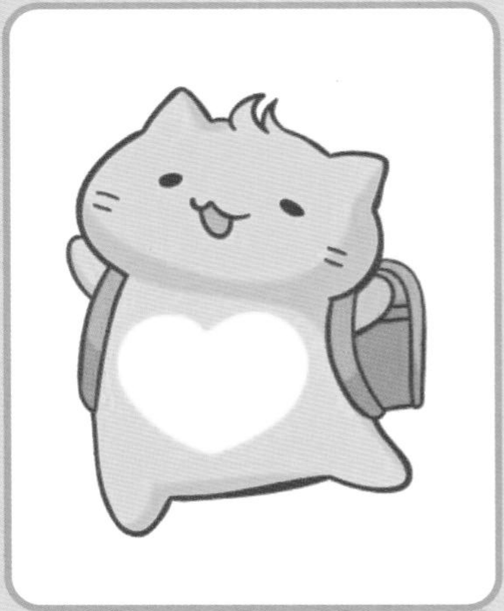

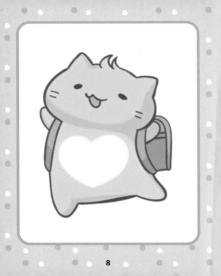

Mitchy

He's a cat who loves to spend every day lazing around. He doesn't go to school, but he loves his backpack.

- Best features: His cowlick and the heart on his belly.

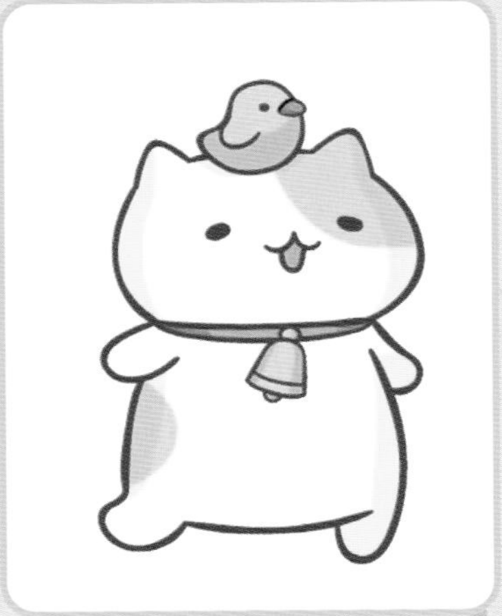

Piyopiyo

He's a cat who's always with his chick. When he rings his cowbell, the chick gives some kind of performance. Rumors say the chick acts as an alarm to both wake and warn him . . . !

Colorful

A cat whose unusual colors make him unique. You'd think he would like things fancy, but his room and belongings are very simple . . . it's because he wants to stand out the most.

Honey

He is a honey bee and loves to fly. Contrary to his appearance, he loves spicy food.

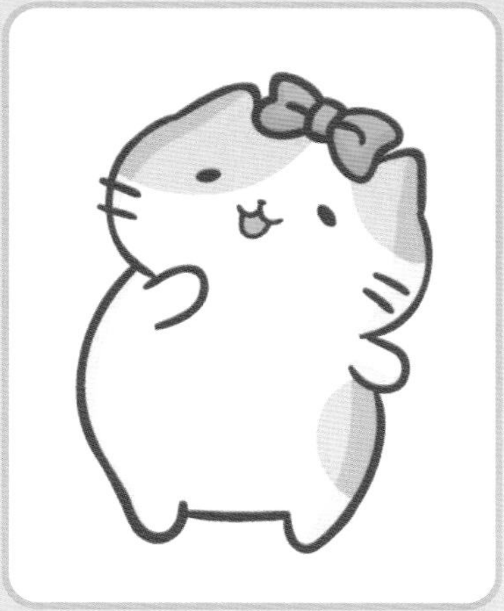

Ribbon

Truly a maiden cat in love, who seems to be interested in a certain other cat. She wears a ribbon for added femininity in order to get the attention of that cat.

- **She is very shy and easily embarrassed.**

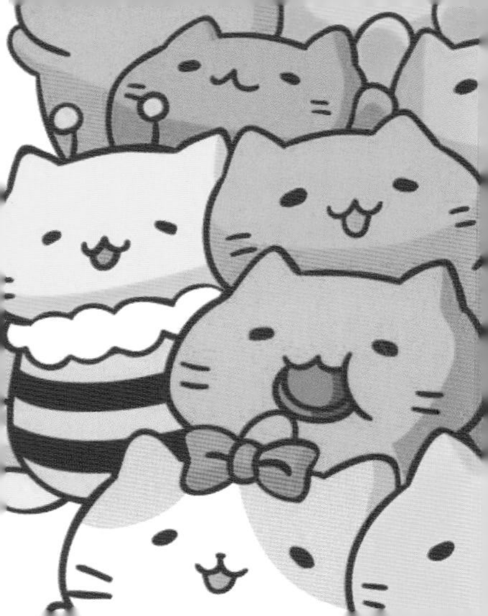

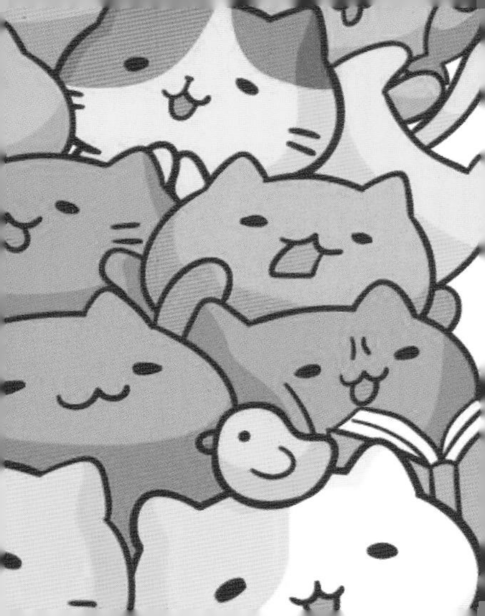

Spring Cleaning

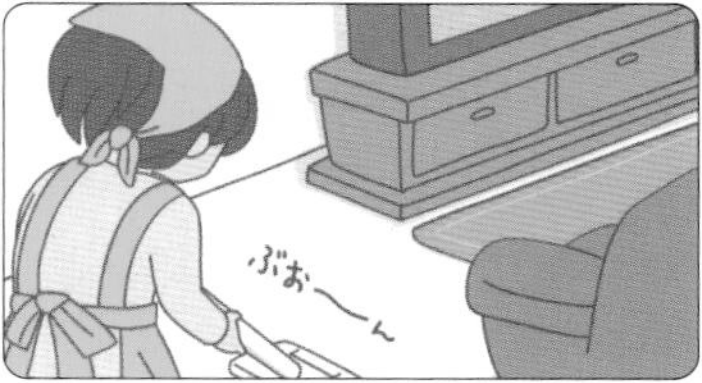
ぶお〜ん

Vrrrm

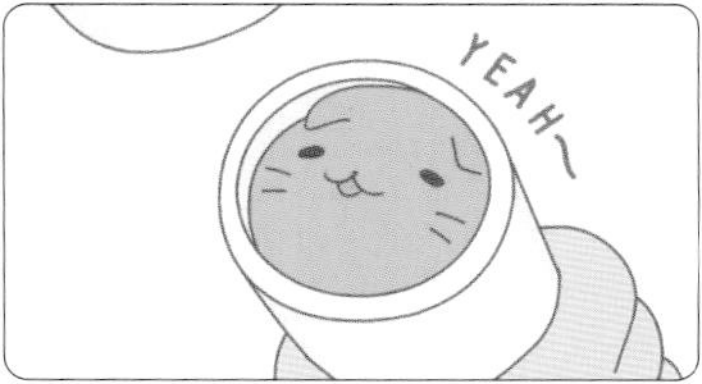
YEAH~

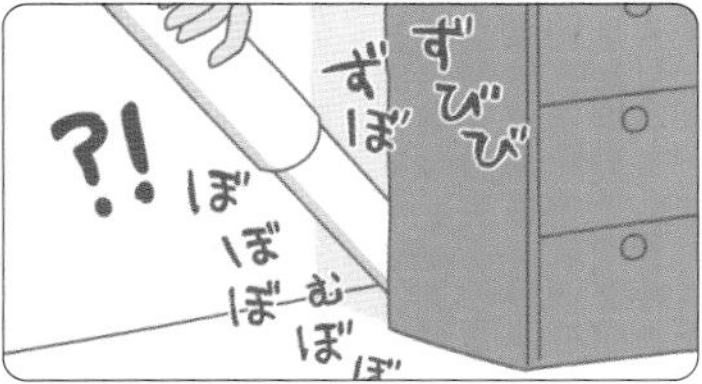
ずびび
ずぼ
?!

Thump Thump Thump Zoop

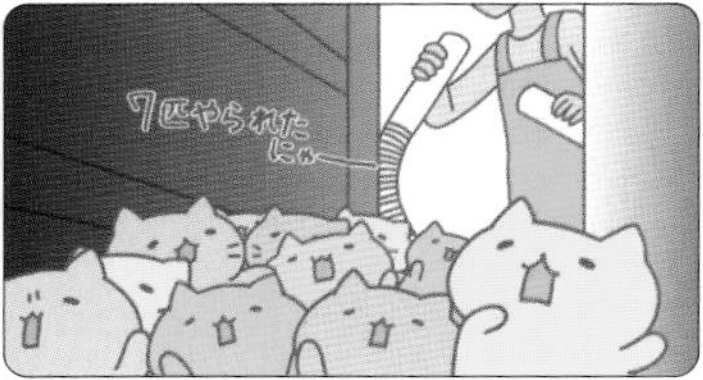
7匹やられたにゃー

It got 7 of us!

Love Shot

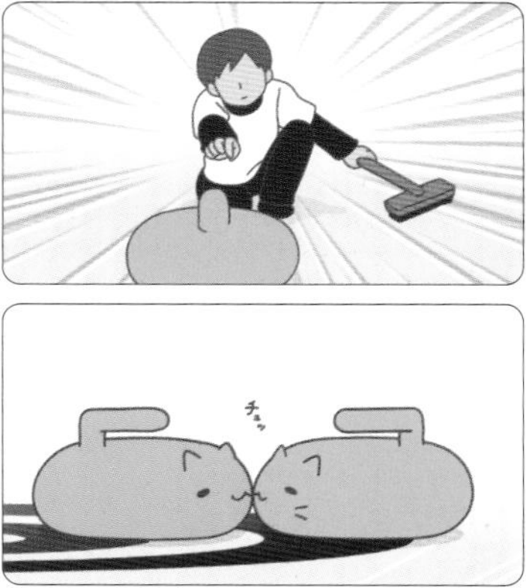
チュッ

Smooch

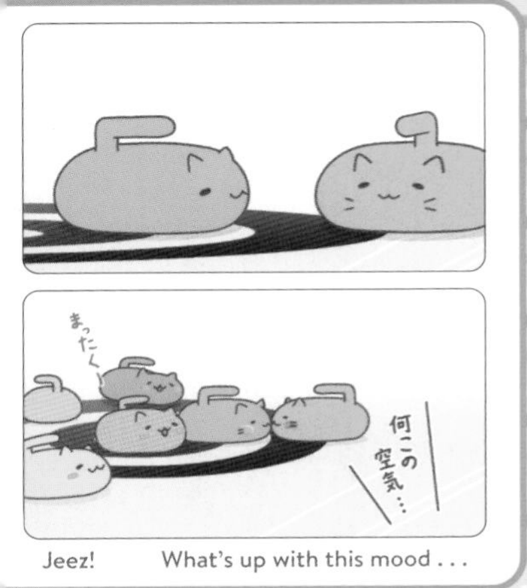
まったく～
何この空気…
Jeez!
What's up with this mood . . .

Confused Deduction

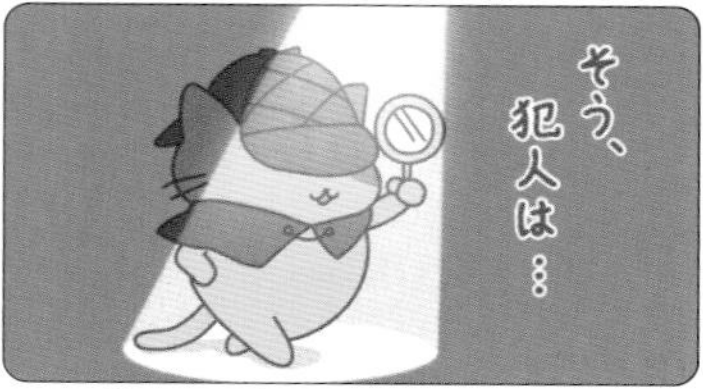
そう、
犯人は…

That's right! The culprit is . . .

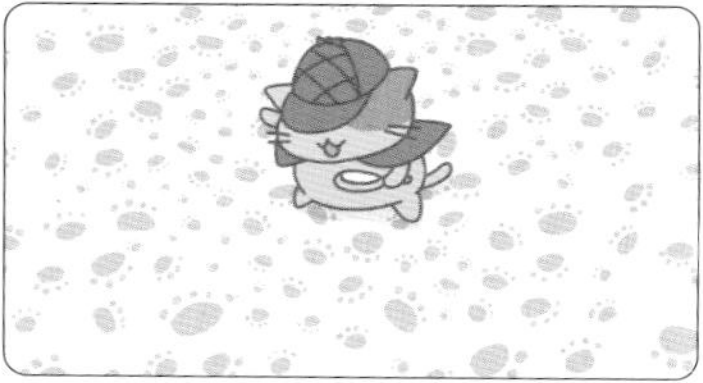

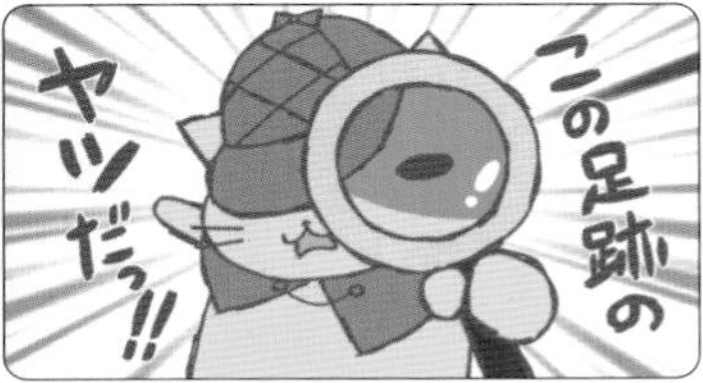
この足跡の
ヤツだっ!!

The one who left this footprint!

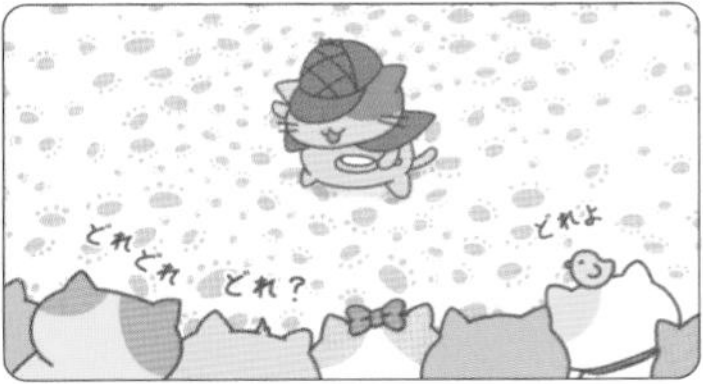
どれどれ
どれ?
どれよ

Yeah? Which? Which one?

Realization

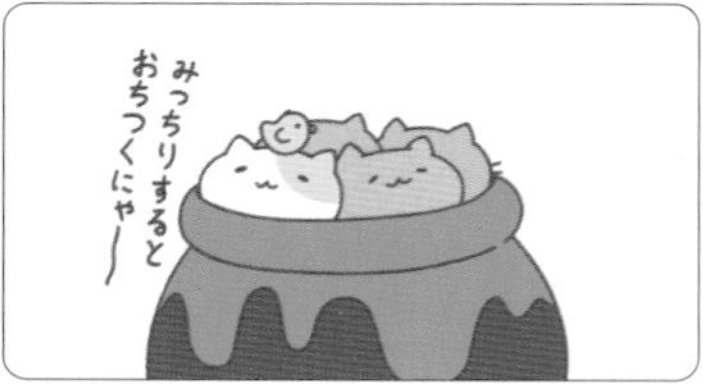
みっちりすると
おちつくにゃ〜

Being all squished together is so relaxing.

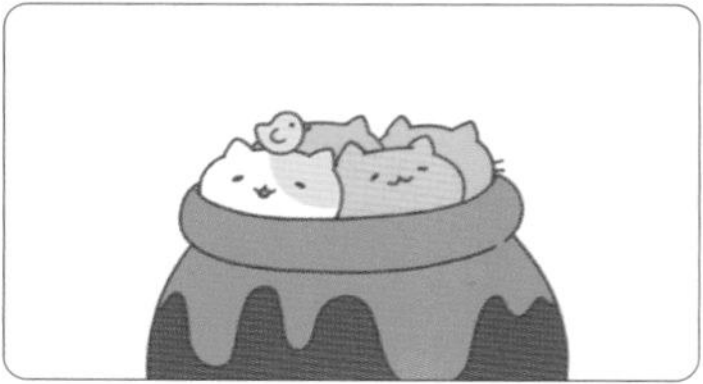

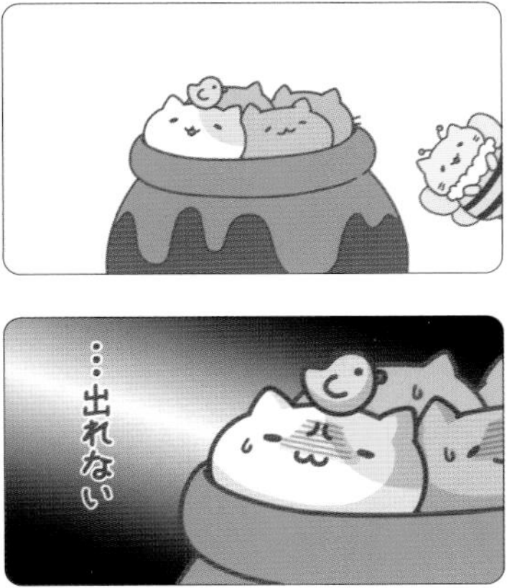
…出れない

. . . I can't get out.

Spontaneous

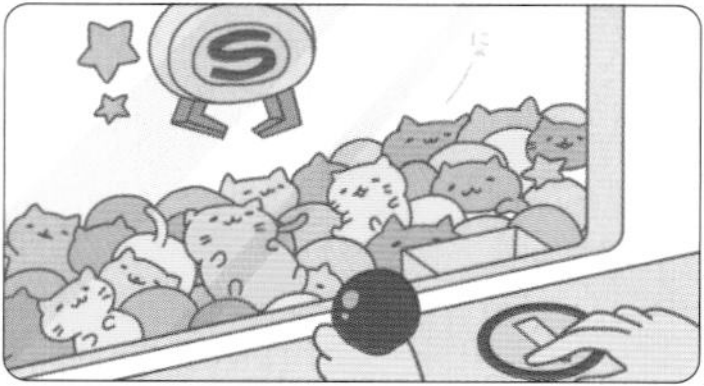
にゃ

Meow

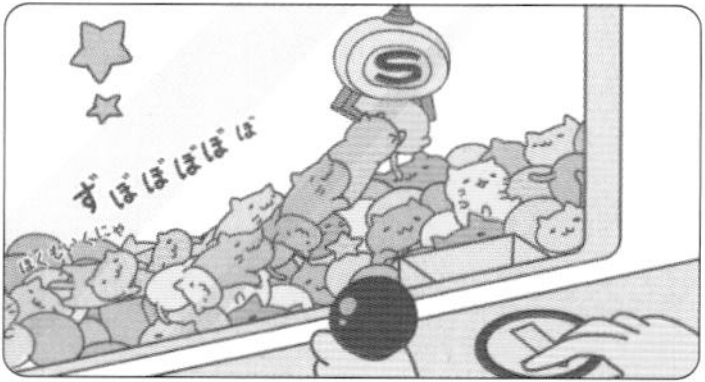
ずぼぼぼぼぼ
ぼくもいくにゃ

I wanna go, too.   Jam Jam Jam

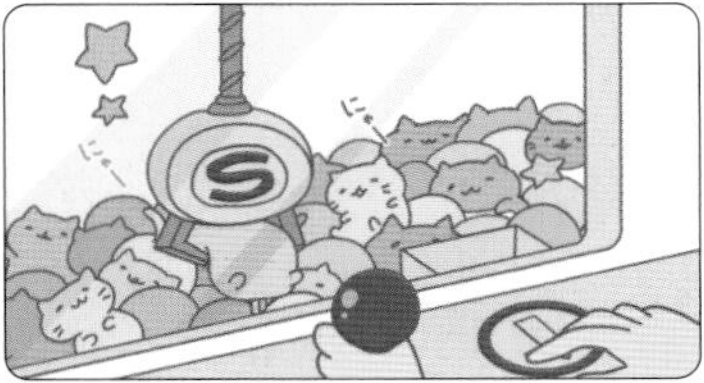
にゃー
にゃー
S

Meow Meow

Um . . .

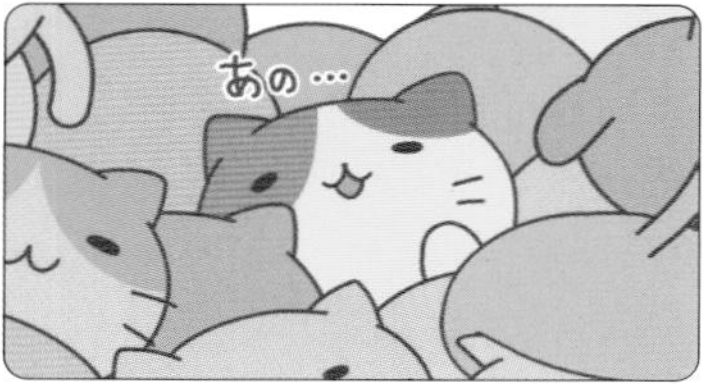
あの…

Um . . .

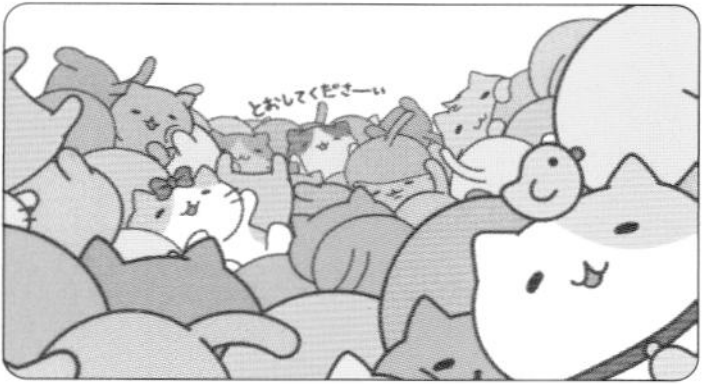
とおしてくださーい

Please let me through . . .

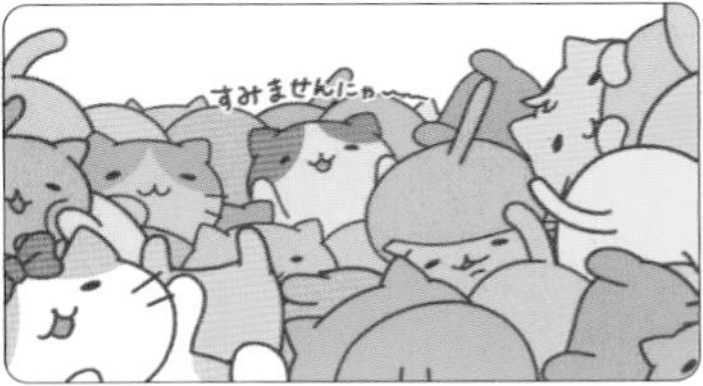
すみませんにゃ〜〜

Excuse meow . . .

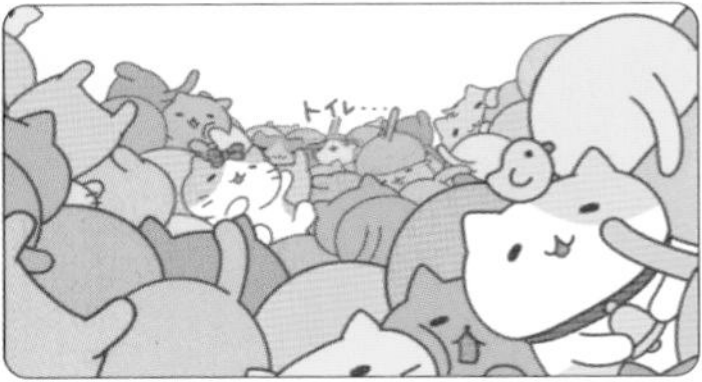
トイレ・・・

Bathroom, please . . .

This book has been bound using
handcraft methods and
Smyth-sewn to ensure durability.

Text was written by Anime-MitchiriNeko.

The interior was designed by Josh McDonnell.